Put Beginning Readers on the Right Track with
ALL ABOARD READING™

The All Aboard Reading series is especially for beginning readers. Written by noted authors and illustrated in full color, these are books that children really and truly *want* to read—books to excite their imagination, tickle their funny bone, expand their interests, and support their feelings. With five different reading levels, All Aboard Reading lets you choose which books are most appropriate for your children and their growing abilities.

Picture Readers
Picture Readers have super-simple texts, with many nouns appearing as rebus pictures. At the end of each book are 24 flash cards—on one side is the rebus picture; on the other side is the written-out word.

Pre-Level 1
First Friends, First Readers have a super-simple text starring lovable recurring characters. Each book features two easy stories that will hold the attention of even the youngest reader while promoting an early sense of accomplishment.

Level 1
Level 1 books have very few lines per page, very large type, easy words, lots of repetition, and pictures with visual "cues" to help children figure out the words on the page.

Level 2
Level 2 books are printed in slightly smaller type than Level 1 books. The stories are more complex, but there is still lots of repetition in the text, and many pictures. The sentences are quite simple and are broken up into short lines to make reading easier.

Level 3
Level 3 books have considerably longer texts, harder words, and more complicated sentences.

All Aboard for happy reading!

To my favorite golfer: my mom—A.G.

Text copyright © 2002 by Andrew Gutelle. All rights reserved. Published by Grosset &
Dunlap, a division of Penguin Putnam Books for Young Readers, 345 Hudson Street, New
York, NY 10014. ALL ABOARD READING and GROSSET & DUNLAP are trademarks of
Penguin Putnam Inc. Published simultaneously in Canada. Printed in the U.S.A.

Library of Congress Cataloging-in-Publication Data is available.

ISBN 0-448-42663-3 (pbk) A B C D E F G H I J

ISBN 0-448-42664-1 (GB) A B C D E F G H I J

ALL
ABOARD
READING™
Level 3

Tiger Woods

By Andrew Gutelle
with photographs

Grosset & Dunlap • New York

Training a Tiger

Even before he could walk or talk, Tiger Woods could hit a golf ball.

Tiger's dad, Earl Woods, discovered his son's amazing talent. Earl loved golf. He practiced whenever he could. Earl even strung up netting in his garage and worked on his golf swing by hitting balls into the net.

Earl wanted to practice golf, but he also wanted to be with Tiger. So he took his son out to the garage. Baby Tiger sat in his high chair. He watched his dad swing, the way some babies watch TV.

He was fascinated.

One day Tiger was out of his high chair. He stood up holding a tiny club that Earl had cut down to his size. Tiger swung. He hit a golf ball into the net. Earl was delighted. He was no longer the only golfer in the family!

Eldrick "Tiger" Woods was born on December 30, 1975. His mother Kultida named

Tiger at 11 months old

him. Kultida took the "E" from Earl's name and the "K" from her name and made up a name for her son: Eldrick Woods.

Earl nicknamed his son "Tiger." Earl had been a soldier in Vietnam. He was part of a top fighting force called the Green Berets. One of Earl's friends was a South Vietnamese soldier named Vuong Dang Phong. Earl called his friend Tiger because he was very brave. He called his son Tiger to honor his friend.

Many people think of Tiger as an African-American, but that is not quite true. Earl is African-American. Kultida or Tida, as people call her, is Asian. Tiger is a blend of different races.

Tiger grew up in a small house in Cypress, California. He had lots of toys. But his favorite thing to play with was his golf club. Tiger toddled around the house, swinging his club and hitting different balls with it. Soon Earl made Tiger a set of clubs. He cut down three of his old irons and a putter. Tiger carried them in a small red golf bag made by his mother.

Earl took Tiger to the driving range to practice. He hit golf balls by the bucketful. He also learned to putt. Earl often played at the Navy Golf Course. When he took Tiger there, his son played nine holes—half the course—and shot a 48! In golf, the lower the score, the better. Most adult golfers would be thrilled with a nine-hole score below 50. Tiger was only three years old, and he shot a 48!

One day, Earl was told that his three-year-old son couldn't play the Navy course. Club rules said he had to be ten. Earl was not happy with this decision. He needed to find a place

Tiger at one and a half years old

where his son would be welcome.

Earl took Tiger to the Heartwell Golf Park in Long Beach, California. At first, teaching pro Rudy Duran thought Tiger was too young to learn to play golf. But Earl asked Rudy to give his son a chance.

Tiger stepped up to the ball. His tiny hands couldn't grip the club the way a golfer does. So he held it like a baseball bat.

Tiger swung and sent the golf ball flying. He hit seven in a row. Rudy watched the way Tiger stood. He saw his smooth swing. He knew that Tiger was special. Rudy said that he could play there.

For the next few years, Tiger spent many hours at Heartwell. Sometimes his mom drove him there and dropped Tiger off. Rudy helped to coach Tiger and kept an eye on him. Tida would return later, after her son had played eighteen holes.

By the time he was five, Tiger scored in the 90s on an eighteen-hole golf course. He appeared on a television show called *That's Incredible!* Tiger was only in kindergarten. But he was already becoming a star.

Tiger at three years old

Role Models and Idols

One day, eight-year-old Tiger Woods was playing golf with his dad. As Tiger swung his club, Earl coughed loudly. He jingled his keys in his pocket. He dropped his golf bag. Why was Earl trying to distract Tiger? Well, Earl knew that Tiger had worked hard learning to play the game of golf. Now Earl wanted Tiger to work on his mental game.

As a young man, Earl had learned to be mentally strong. He was the only African-American baseball player in his entire college conference. Earl was a star catcher. Some fans and players said awful things to him simply because of his race. Earl learned to block out their remarks and just concentrate on his game.

Earl knew that Tiger might face some of the same cruel comments. Many of the golf courses where Tiger was playing were on country-club grounds. And most of the members of those country clubs were white. Tiger would look out of place to them. Not everyone would welcome him. Earl wanted Tiger to be able to tune out things around him. Tiger needed to do this to play his best.

Tiger's mom also helped him learn self-control. Tida practiced the Buddhist religion. In her culture, people did not brag or get upset in public. Tida helped teach Tiger to remain calm.

Tiger was a typical California kid. He went to public school. He liked the beach. He watched TV and played video games. He ate fast food. Tiger always did his homework. Tida set the rules in the house. Homework came before everything, even golf.

Golf took up all of Tiger's spare time. When he wasn't practicing, he was playing in tournaments. Tiger was often the youngest golfer at these tournaments. The older kids were bigger and stronger. Even so, Tiger usually won. His first big victory was the Optimist International Junior World. He was eight years old. In fact, Tiger won the same championship the next year, too.

Tiger's parents were his role models. But his idol was Jack Nicklaus. Jack was a top college and amateur golfer. He won one hundred

Tiger and Jack Nicklaus

tournaments as pro. But his greatest feat of all

was winning the career Grand Slam.

To capture a Grand Slam a player must win

each of golf's four greatest tournaments during

his career. The four tournaments are the Masters, the U.S. Open, the British Open, and the PGA Championship. Golfers call these important events "majors."

Winning one major is a great achievement. Winning all four is an incredible one. Only four players in golf history had ever done it. Nicklaus completed his Grand Slam at the age of twenty-six. He was the youngest player to win a Grand Slam. He went on to win eighteen major titles—the most ever! No wonder he was said to be golf's greatest champion!

Tiger hung posters of Nicklaus in his room. There was also a chart. It listed Jack's achievements by age. Tiger added a column for his own achievements. So far he had beaten most of Jack's scores when he was a boy. For

example, Jack was twelve when he first shot a round below 80. Tiger had done this by age eight!

By the time he was eleven, Tiger's house was filling up with trophies. He entered thirty tournaments that year in Southern California. He won them all.

One of Tiger's sweetest victories was not in a tournament. It happened on November 28, 1987. Tiger was playing against his dad. As they headed to the final holes, Tiger had the lower score. Earl was an excellent golfer. He had never lost to his son. And he did not want to lose now!

Earl went all out. He averaged par for eighteen holes. Par is the number of golf shots you are supposed to need to finish each hole.

Par would be good enough to win on most

days. But Tiger's eighteen-hole round included four birdies. A birdie is one shot below par. The birdies pushed Tiger's total below Earl's.

Tiger had finally beaten his dad! Even though Earl didn't like losing, he was proud of his son. He believed that Tiger was going to be the greatest golfer of all time!

Tiger with his dad and mom

Tiger Goes to College

In the fall of 1994, the Stanford University golf team was on the road. A tall, skinny freshman carried their bags. That night he would get stuck sleeping on the worst hotel bed. He had books to read. He had homework to do. Welcome to college, Tiger!

Tiger chose Stanford University for two reasons. First of all, it had a fine golf team. Plus, it was one of the best schools in the country. Tiger wanted to win a college golf championship. He also planned to stay in school four years and graduate.

Before he started college, Tiger won his first U.S. Amateur Championship. His victory was big news. Tiger was the youngest winner ever. And he was the first minority champion.

Tiger was a celebrity in the golf world. But at college he was just another freshman. Stanford was a great school. Every student had one special talent or another. For once Tiger could just blend into the crowd. He loved it!

Tiger was the only freshman on the golf team. The seniors playfully teased him. They kidded him about his glasses. They laughed at the way he danced. They made joke phone calls to his hotel room.

On the golf course, Tiger had always been on his own. Now he was part of a team. Tiger quickly fit in. He won his first college tournament. While still a freshman, he became the top-ranked student golfer in the country.

As U.S. Amateur champ, Tiger was invited to play in some pro tournaments. But he had to follow rules set down by the National Collegiate Athletic Association. The NCAA supervised college athletes. According to their rules, Tiger could not collect prize money. But he could still play and test his skills against the world's greatest golfers.

Tiger played in the 1995 Masters. He finished with the top score of any amateur. During summer vacation Tiger competed in the U.S. Open and the British Open. With each tournament he gained valuable experience. He was learning what it would take to win as a pro.

In the fall Tiger returned to Stanford. Tiger worked hard and maintained a fine 3.0 grade average. But the NCAA had many confusing rules. It was getting tougher for Tiger to balance college and golf.

One day, golf legend Arnold Palmer visited Tiger at school. They went out together. At dinner they talked about golf. Tiger was a college student on a tight budget. So Arnie paid the check.

The next day, Tiger was suspended from the team. NCAA rules do not allow students to receive gifts from pro players. Was the dinner a gift? To remove any doubt, Tiger sent a check to Palmer. He was put back on the team the next day. But Tiger was angry. He felt that the rules were not fair. He began to think more and more about leaving college.

Tiger won the NCAA golf championship as a sophomore. Then, in the summer, he went to the Pumpkin Ridge Golf Club near Portland, Oregon. Tiger had already defended his U.S. Amateur title one time. Now he would try again. No one had ever won three Amateurs in a row.

Once again Tiger made it to the finals. His opponent was Steve Scott, a college student from the University of Florida. They would play thirty-six holes—two whole rounds—head-to-head. The winner at the end of the day would be the new champion.

In the morning, Scott surged ahead. He led by five strokes with sixteen holes to go. Tiger had rallied to win his first two Amateurs. He would have to do it again.

Tiger stormed back. Scott played very well. Still his lead began to slowly shrink. The deciding moment came on the next to last hole. Tiger faced a tricky thirty-five-foot putt. He sent his ball rolling across the green and into the cup! The crowd exploded. Tiger pumped his fist. Scott sagged a bit as he watched the scene. Tiger went on to win the title.

A few days after the match, on August 28, 1996, Tiger held a press conference. He had talked to his parents. Tiger promised them that

Tiger celebrates after scoring an eagle during
the U.S. Amateur

one day he would finish college. But he had

made up his mind. It was time to turn pro.

"Hello, world," he said with a smile.

Tigermania

"Playing in his first tournament as a professional, would you please welcome Tiger Woods."

Tiger was an amateur a week ago. Now he stood at the first tee of the Greater Milwaukee Open. He was about to play for the first time as a pro. The fans cheered. Tiger smiled. He was on his way.

Tiger wanted to join the Professional Golfers' Association, or PGA. Each year the PGA sets up a schedule of tournaments. The schedule began in January. Tiger turned pro in

September of 1996. He had missed most of this year's tour. He had to catch up fast!

Tiger planned to play in seven events. He wanted to qualify for next year's tour. To do so, he needed to play well. He must be one of the top 125 money-winners *for the whole year*.

Tiger was already a wealthy young man. After turning pro, he had signed a contract with Nike. He would wear their clothes, and they would pay him millions of dollars. But that money didn't matter here. Only money earned on the tour counted.

Tiger finished tied for 60th in the Greater Milwaukee Open. He earned a check for $2,544. Tiger was thrilled. "That's my money," he said, proudly. "I earned this!"

As the weeks passed, Tiger got better and better. He won his fourth event, the Las Vegas

Invitational. Two weeks later he won again. Tiger finished the year ranked 24th in earnings. He easily qualified for next year!

Tiger brought a new energy to golf. When he played, an event sold out. Young people bought tickets. So did African-Americans and other minorities. They followed Tiger around the course. Millions of more people watched on TV. Many were new golf fans. People gave this excitement a name. They called it "Tigermania."

Tiger tees off as the crowd at the 1997 Masters looks on

Tiger assists an aspiring golfer

After the season, Tiger set up a charity. It was called the Tiger Woods Foundation. Tiger would give golf clinics for inner city kids. He would also raise money for charity. In a letter, Tiger explained his goals for young people. "Do your best. Play fairly. Embrace every activity with integrity, honesty, and discipline. And above all, have fun."

Master of Augusta

On April 10, 1997, the world's best golfers gathered in Augusta, Georgia. They were there to play in the first major tournament of the year—the Masters. One of the favorites to win was twenty-one-year-old Tiger Woods.

This was Tiger's first major since turning pro. A win here would make history. Tiger would be the Masters' youngest champion. He would also be the first minority to win.

For a long time golf had been a segregated sport. Black players were not allowed on the PGA tour. The only blacks on many courses were caddies. They carried golf bags for the white players.

In 1961, the "whites only" rule changed. Still the Augusta National Golf Club stuck to the old ways. It wasn't until 1975 that a black golfer played in the Masters. His name was Lee Elder.

Golfing legend Lee Elder

Tiger was only the fourth African-American to play the Masters. He knew about the problems of race. As a boy, he had not been allowed to play at some country clubs. He even received hate mail while at Stanford. Tiger understood what a Masters win would mean. It would be a huge achievement. Tiger would finish the job started by black golfers like Elder, Charlie Sifford, and Ted Rhodes.

Tiger played round one with defending champ Nick Faldo. A huge gallery of fans was waiting at the first hole. Tiger set his golf ball on the tee. He swung. There was a loud *CRACK!* as golf club and ball met. The ball rocketed forward. Tiger hoped to hit his shot down the fairway—the grassy stretch between the tee and the hole. But his ball went to the left. Way left. It flew into the pine trees. Tiger was in trouble!

Tiger finished the first hole one over par. A bogey! He quickly added three more bogeys. Tiger shot 40 on the front nine holes. If he wanted to win he had to get going—now!

Tiger shortened his backswing. It was a risky move. A golfer usually needs hours, even days, of practice to correct his swing. But somehow

Tiger got it right. His next shot sailed down the middle of the fairway.

Tiger birdied that hole. He birdied three others. Tiger even added a two-under-par eagle. And no more bogeys! Tiger shot 70 for the day. He was in fourth place.

Tiger was still in a groove the next day. He scored a sizzling 66. It was the best second-round score. Tiger did even better one day later. He shot a 65. After three rounds, he had a nine-shot lead. The other golfers were stunned.

Could anyone catch him? Colin Montgomerie had played round three with Tiger. "There's no chance humanly possible," he said.

On Sunday, Tiger prepared for his final round. He stood in the practice area working on his swing. A man approached to wish him luck. Tiger looked up. It was Lee Elder.

"I was part of history by being the first black to play here," Elder said later. "I had to be part of history by watching Tiger be the first black to win here."

Tiger did not disappoint Elder. As he reached the final hole, he led by twelve shots. One more par would give him a four-round total of 270. That would be a record low score.

Tiger's tee shot hooked left, but he quickly recovered. His next swing landed his ball on the green. Tiger marched up the fairway. The crowd clapped and cheered. Smiling, Tiger gave fans high-fives as he walked past them.

The applause grew as he reached the green. Two shots later he sank his final putt. Tiger had the win. He had the record low score. He had his place in golf history.

Tiger hugged his caddie Mike "Fluff" Cowan. Then he found his mother and father in the crowd. He hugged them, too. "My father told me last night this will probably be the toughest round I ever have to play, but it could be the most rewarding," Tiger said later. "And he was right."

Tiger receives his Masters jacket from Nick Faldo

Streaking to a Slam

Tiger was the master of Augusta. He hit the ball farther than anyone. He rolled in putt after putt. Tiger was thrilled with his win. But he was not satisfied. He thought that he could play better!

A few weeks after the Masters, Tiger returned to the practice range. He worked with swing coach Butch Harmon. Tiger

Tiger and Butch

was seeking more control over the distance of each shot. That would help him make better shots from tricky spots on the golf course.

Butch changed the way Tiger drew back his club. Tiger worked very hard on his new swing. On some days he hit more than a thousand golf balls.

Tiger also changed his diet. He cut down on cheeseburgers and fries and started eating healthier foods. Tiger lifted weights. He exercised. He wanted to add muscle and build up his strength.

Meanwhile, Tiger played the PGA Tour. He was still learning to control his new swing. He won one more tournament in 1997. He won one time the next year.

In 1999, Tiger made another change. He hired Steve Williams as his new caddie. Tiger

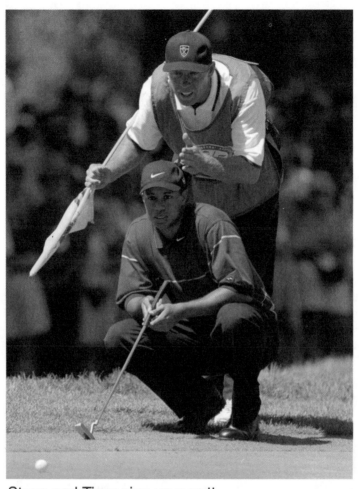
Steve and Tiger size up a putt

wanted someone that fit his hard-working style.
Stevie, as he is known, had been a caddie—"on
the bag"—for top golfers like Greg Norman.
Now he would be an important member of
Tiger's team.

Meanwhile, Tiger kept practicing and playing. Someday all the hard work would pay off.
Finally, in the summer of 1999 it did. Tiger's
golf game went from very good to awesome.
Over a stretch of ten tournaments, he won
seven. One of his wins was the PGA
Championship—his second major.

Tiger finished 1999 with four straight wins.
The next year, he kept winning. In Hawaii, he
defeated Ernie Els in a playoff. Five straight! In
California he erased a seven-stroke lead and
won again. Six straight! It was the longest winning streak that any golfer had had in fifty-two
years.

Finally the streak ended. So Tiger set his
sights on another goal. So far, he had won a
Masters and a PGA Championship in his brief
career. Now he wanted to capture the U.S. and

British Opens. Those four wins would make him the youngest Grand Slam champ ever.

The U.S. Open took place at Pebble Beach, California. Pebble Beach featured the world's largest water hazard—the Pacific Ocean. It was one of the toughest golf courses in the world.

Tiger takes a shot at Pebble Beach

Tiger shot a scorching 65 to take the first-round lead. As he waited to start round two, he heard a huge roar. It was coming from the eighteenth green. Jack Nicklaus was finishing his last Open. His fans were saying goodbye. "It would have been nice seeing it," Tiger said later. "But I had more important things to take care of."

Tiger led after one round. Now he made great shot after great shot. After three rounds he had an incredible ten-stroke lead! On the last day Tiger began his victory march. He shot par on each of the first nine holes. That's all he needed with such a big lead. He was cruising. But the huge crowd wanted more. They waited eagerly for some Tiger magic.

Suddenly, on the tenth hole, the fans got their wish. Tiger rolled in an eighteen-foot

birdie putt. He parred eleven. Then he birdied three straight holes. He was on track for another sizzling score.

Tiger finished with a four-round total of 272. That tied Nicklaus and Lee Janzen for the lowest U.S. Open total ever. One of the fans at

The first green at the majestic "Old Course"

the final hole held up a sign that said it all: "Thank you, Jack. Long live Tiger."

Five weeks later Tiger was in St. Andrews, Scotland. He had come to play in the British Open. One more win and his Grand Slam quest would be complete.

St. Andrews was the perfect place to make history. Golf had been played there for five hundred years. The famous "Old Course" was the world's first eighteen-hole golf course.

Tiger played at St. Andrews once before. It was in the 1995 British Open. He loved the challenge of the Old Course. "Every time I play it, I learn something new about the golf course," he said.

Once again, Tiger took charge. In the first three rounds, he shot 67, 66, and 67. Tiger had a six-stroke lead. David Duval was in

second place. He would play with Tiger in the
final round. Duval was playing well. He was
eager to meet the challenge. "I'm excited," he
said. "How could I not be?"

Tiger was eighteen holes from history. Or

Duvall and Tiger pose after the Showdown at Sherwood, 1999

was he? Duval birdied four of the first seven holes. He cut Tiger's lead in half.

The 379-yard tenth hole turned out to be crucial. Tiger hit a mammoth tee shot that rolled onto the green. After Duval missed a birdie, Tiger made his. His lead started to grow again.

Tiger was eight shots ahead as he reached the last hole. Officials had to hold back the crowd. Tiger marched to the green. He finished the tournament with a score of 19 under par. Not only was that the best score in British Open history, it was the greatest four-round total ever at St. Andrews. The career Grand Slam was his.

"It's really hard to put into words the emotions and feelings going through me," said Tiger afterward. "To complete the Slam at St.

Andrews, where golf all started, makes it even more special."

Tiger proudly holding the claret jug

What Next?

On April 8, 2001, Tiger did it again. His eighteen-foot birdie on the final hole clinched his second Masters. For a moment even Tiger was stunned. He pulled his cap over his forehead to hide the tears in his eyes.

Tiger now held all four major titles at the same time. He had won six majors in all. Jack Nicklaus collected eighteen during his pro career. Tiger has a chance to catch and pass his idol. It will take years to do it.

Will Tiger end up the greatest golfer ever? "I hope so," he said. "What I truly hope is that the best I can be will be good enough to become that. Who knows? I'll keep working."